Lyveden New Bield

Northamptonshire

THE NATIONAL TRUST

Above Sir Thomas Tresham in 1568. His armour is decorated with trefoils, the three-leaved clover symbol which he adopted as his personal emblem (Collection of the Duke of Buccleuch)

Right The grand classical doorway in the north wing announces the formal entrance to the New Bield

AN INTERRUPTED DREAM

'Hard to say whether greater his delight or skill in buildings, though more forward in beginning than fortunate in finishing his fabrics.' THOMAS FULLER ON SIR THOMAS TRESHAM (*Worthies of England*, 1662)

'Sir Thomas Tresham's delight, skill and misfortunes are all epitomised in Lyveden New Bield. When one first sees its skeleton silhouetted against the skyline in the distant view from the Oundle–Brigstock road, it looks less like an Elizabethan ruin than a house interrupted in the process of building. And that in fact is what it is. When Tresham died in September 1605, the masons laid down their tools, never to take them up again. There the lodge still stands in suspended animation.' MARK GIROUARD

Above Tresham's coat of arms, which features his trefoil emblem

Below The New Bield from the south-west

Lyveden's isolated position, together with the superb quality of the craftsmanship that created it, has resulted in a unique building almost unaltered since Tudor times. It was designed to serve as a garden lodge, to be approached through orchards, terraces and canals, and to be enjoyed as a place of pleasure and secret worship.

Both house and garden, therefore, present themselves as an interrupted dream, an unfinished symphony, a grand plan suspended for ever by a change of fortune and the turn of personal and historical events.

Fortunately, the circumstances which led to the ruin of the Tresham family and the abandonment of the New Bield before completion, also led to the almost inadvertent preservation of crucial family papers. Notes, letters and accounts of Sir Thomas Tresham were concealed in the walls of Rushton Hall after his son, Francis, was identified as a conspirator in the Gunpowder Plot. These papers, discovered in 1832 and recently partly transcribed, offer fascinating insights into building design and plantsmanship in the late Elizabethan period. Underlying all this is Tresham's adherence to the Catholic faith, at a time when Catholicism was seen as a serious threat to the Crown.

'As it is upon the north side, so must that be on the south side and all the other sides from the garden wall to the lodge.' SIR THOMAS TRESHAM, 1597

Above Tresham was persecuted by Elizabeth I for his Catholic faith, but she shared his fascination with signs and symbols, as the skirt in this portrait of the Queen makes clear

Right The New Bield was planned as a symmetrical Greek cross

Until 1594 the 14th-century manor house at Lyveden – the Old Bield (or Old Building) – stood within a small, enclosed garden. Sir Thomas Tresham planned to extend the garden southwards up towards the ridge of the valley where he designed a garden lodge, Lyveden New Bield (or New Building).

Built in the shape of a Greek cross with four equal arms, the New Bield is perfectly symmetrical and precisely proportioned. The building design draws heavily on Tresham's knowledge and from his extensive architectural library.

Tresham had already demonstrated his interest in designing extraordinary and complex buildings with his Triangular Lodge at Rushton. There he had used a repetition of the number three to represent the Trinity of God the Father, Son and Holy Ghost. At Lyveden, in addition he took the numbers five, symbolising the wounds of Christ on the cross, and seven to symbolise the seven instruments of the Passion (Crucifixion).

The plan of the New Bield consists of five equal squares. Each arm of the Cross ends in a bay with five sides each measuring five feet, making a total of 25 feet. This is no accident – the 25th is the date of both the Nativity (December) and the Annunciation (March). The need for such precise complexity may appear baffling today, but it was typical of the Elizabethan love of ingenious riddles.

The lodge is on three floors: the basement for servants, the ground and first floors for entertaining. Outside, sets of three shields are divided by three windows, diamonds are grouped in threes, and the measurement from one side of the building to the other is 243 feet – three x three x three x three x three!

The carved frieze between the ground and first floor is based on the Italian architect Serlio's pattern books, adapted by Tresham to show seven emblems of the Passion of Christ. The Greek letters IHS (meaning Jesus) and XP (for Christ) occur most prominently, repeated in the middle of each side of each bay and in the middle of each side of the arms of the cross.

The frieze above the first floor bears Latin inscriptions. These once continued around the entire building, although now only part survives. The texts are taken from the Vulgate, the Latin version of the Bible, juggled to fit the spaces around the building, with the words IESVS (Jesus) and MARIA (Mary) occurring either side of each bay window and emphasised by the Tresham emblem, the trefoil (three-leaved clover).

IESVS.MVNDI.SALVS.–.GAVDE.MATER.VIRGO.MARIA.–[.VERBVM.]AVTEM.CRVCIS.
PERENTIBVS.QVIDE[M.STVLTITIA.EST.–.IESVS.BEATVS.]VENTER.QVI.TE.PORTAVIT.–
[.MARIA.VIRGO.SPONSA.INNVPTA.]…[BENEDIXI]T.TE.DEVS.IN.AE[TERNVM.MARIA.–
.MIHI.AVTEM.A]BSIT.GLORIARI.NISI.IN.CRVCE.DOMINI.NOSTRI.XP.

Top Complex religious symbols similar to those on the New Bield fill this 1585 portrait of Tresham

Above and left The frieze between the ground and first floors is carved with roundels symbolising the Passion of Christ

Jesus the Salvation of the World – rejoice, O Mother Virgin Mary – But the Word of His Cross is foolishness even to those perishing – Jesus, blessed is the womb that bore thee – Mary, Virgin, unwedded spouse … God blessed thee for ever, O Mary – God forbid that I should glory save in the Cross of our Lord Christ.

The sacred monogram IHS is formed by the pillar, cross with crown of thorns, ladder, sponge and spear, with heart between them, a cord (or scourge) in the form of an S, and three nails below. This emblem forms the first three Greek letters of the name Jesus, and was adopted as the symbol of the Jesuits. The surrounding band contains the Tresham trefoil and the Latin words '*mihi esto*' ('to me be it').

XP forms the first two Greek letters of the name Christ (or *Chi Rho*), which also stands for *Christos resurrexit* – 'Christ has risen'. The surrounding laurel wreath is embossed with the Greek initials ETN, for 'εν τουτω νικη', meaning 'victory in this'.

Surrounded by a twisted cord are the lantern, torches, swords and spears used during the arrest of Jesus in the Garden of Gethsemane. On the right-hand sabre is the ear of Malchus cut off by Peter at the arrest of Jesus.

Thirty pieces of silver surround Judas's money bag, which is tied to form a trefoil.

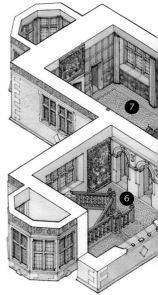

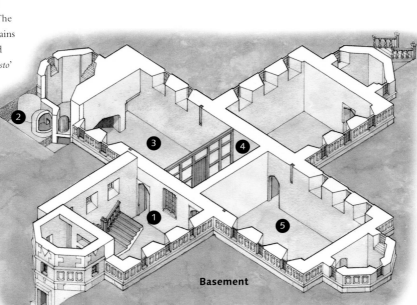

Basement

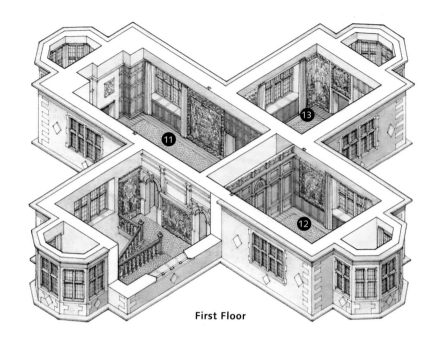

First Floor

1   Staircase Hall
2   Ovens
3   Kitchen
4   Dry Larder
5   Buttery
6   Landing
7   Hall
8   Parlour
9   Entrance Lobby
10 Porch
11 Great Chamber
12 Bedchamber
13 Best Bedchamber

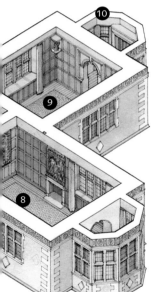

Ground Floor

The scourge, pillar, crown of thorns and sceptre of reeds, surrounded by a band of twisted linen. On the pillar stands a cockerel, which Jesus said would only crow after Peter had denied Him three times.

Three dice, each showing the number five, surround the seamless garment of Jesus, contained within a ring of Roman helmets and gauntlets. This represents the casting of lots by the soldiers to own the garment.

The crown of thorns surrounds the cross, with ladder, spear, sponge, hammer and pincers alongside.

'The said leaning place (lodgement table, or by what name so ever it is properly to be termed) I would have a foot in breadth sailing inwards, as whereon to lean.'

SIR THOMAS TRESHAM'S INSTRUCTIONS TO JOHN SLYNNE, 1597

Above The north side of the Staircase Hall. The doorway arches in the basement servants' quarters are of the traditional Tudor form, whereas the grander family rooms above have more elaborate classical doorcases

The Servants' Entrance

Today, you enter the New Bield by the servants' entrance, which lies a little below ground level on the south side. It is probable that this was originally a tunnelled entrance so that the servants could not be seen by any of Tresham's friends walking in the garden. The concealed entrance also meant that the outline of the building was kept symmetrical above ground level.

Inside the building, it soon becomes apparent that Lyveden was intended to be a fully habitable house, with all the requisites of a gentleman's residence, even if on a relatively small scale. Kitchen, cellar and offices were in the basement; Hall, Parlour and Entrance Lobby on the ground floor. The Great Chamber (the main reception room of an Elizabethan house) was on the first floor, over the Hall, with a withdrawing chamber and best bedchamber adjoining. The southern wing of the cross was taken up by the staircase.

The West Wing

The west wing still retains the main fireplace of the kitchen, behind which are the bake ovens for cooking and the copper for heating water with the open flue above. Cupboard space behind the main fire provided valuable dry storage for salt. Salt was much used in Elizabethan England for preserving meat.

Above the kitchen is the Hall, which was separated by a screen from the service corridor. Above, the Great Chamber is decorated with superbly finished stonework, particularly

surrounding the entrance off the main staircase.

Throughout the building Tresham adapted conventional design, innovating in many ways. The rainwater pipes and all the flues from the fireplaces, for example, were hidden within the walls. This avoided spoiling the external symmetry of the building, and allowed uninterrupted views from the intended rooftop walk.

The East Wing

In the east wing, the open bay window of the Parlour is decorated with the coats of arms of Tresham and his wife Muriel Throckmorton. As well as providing extra light to the Parlour, the open bay served as a lookout point along the bridleway towards Wadenhoe and the Nene Valley. This provided a welcome element of security for Tresham, a practising Catholic during times of persecution.

The Entrance Doorway

Originally, the building was raised on a mound five feet high and accessed by a flight of steps (again five feet high), to an arched doorway leading in to the north wing of the house. The doorway is carved with fine detail from the pattern books of Serlio and Scamozzi. The main entrance led to a lobby. This led to a room, possibly intended as a chapel, where a niche in the corner still awaits a statue of the Madonna. The precise holes drilled to hold the statue and outer glass casing are still visible.

With the adjoining moats stocked with fish, venison from the surrounding deer-park, and fruit from the extensive orchards, Tresham probably envisaged his garden lodge as an exquisite pleasure pavilion, providing facilities for storing, preparing and consuming lavish meals, with ample accommodation to withdraw to afterwards.

Above **The view into the Buttery from the north wing**

Left **The Staircase Hall from the Buttery. The square recesses would have taken the joists that supported the ground floor**

9

Above Tresham would probably have ornamented the roof with a cupola like this, which was designed by his surveyor Robert Stickells for Hawkfield Lodge, near Rushton, which no longer survives

Right Tresham may have planned to give the New Bield another storey

With additional bedchambers, servants' quarters and sufficient room for a small library, Lyveden moved away from the traditional design of a mere hunting lodge. Tresham himself describes it as 'my garden lodge', a smaller house at the end of the garden, designed to be used as a place of retreat. A similar grand lodge exists at Wothorpe, where William Cecil's household moved, 'when the greater [house] at Burleigh was a-sweeping'.

The New Bield was probably meant to have another storey. A letter written by Tresham in or around April 1604 has normally been taken to refer to work on the Old Bield, but in view of its timing, it is more probably concerned with the New. He gives instructions that work on 'my building at Lyveden', which had apparently been discontinued, is to be prepared on the site in the intervening months; he refers to those two floors as containing both a great chamber and a gallery. It would make sense, in the light of these instructions, if the first floor had been all but completed by the time of his death in September 1605, but the second floor was no further advanced than the assemblage of materials on site.

If one accepts that a gallery floor was intended at the top of the house, the image of the New Bield is radically altered. It becomes a house much higher and more dramatic than the surviving building suggests, especially if a rooftop walkway was to be provided above.

Such extra height was the fashion in the late Elizabethan period – as was the provision of a long gallery, and a flat roof above it, on which to promenade and enjoy the view. At Lyveden the view would have been a splendid one: to the north down across the moats, mounts and terraces of the garden to the Old Bield, and beyond it to the Lyveden deer-park; to the east and west across pastures studded with Tresham's flocks of sheep; to the south over the treetops of Rockingham forest; and on all sides in the distance the billowing expanses of the Northamptonshire landscape.

Above An upper window in the east wing. The New Bield was designed partly as a viewing platform and so is well supplied with windows

Left The New Bield from the south-west

Above Queen Mary, who appointed Sir Thomas Tresham the elder as Grand Prior of the Order of St John of Jerusalem.

Right Sir Thomas Tresham the elder, the grandfather of the builder of Lyveden New Bield. He served in the households of Henry VIII and Edward VI, and, as a Catholic, prospered under Queen Mary

The history of Lyveden (or Lefden, as it was known) dates back far beyond the reign of Elizabeth I and the Treshams. The finding of a Roman temple and artefacts suggests communities were established 1500 years earlier. A strong flowing stream along the valley bottom, with an iron-rich clay soil, made it an ideal site for developing industry. During the 11th century there was iron smelting and later a vibrant medieval pottery industry producing 'lyveden-ware', which was sold throughout the Midlands.

The villages of Magna Lyveden, Potters Lyveden, Great Lyveden and Little Lyveden developed along the valley bottom throughout the 13th and 14th centuries, with a combined population of more than 200 by 1400.

Surrounded by the forests of Rockingham, the Lyveden valley was also rich hunting ground. In 1328 a licence was granted to Robert de Wyville, Bishop of Salisbury, to enclose part of the forest to form a deer-park. The surrounding land was farmed in a three-field system of crop rotation with wheat, barley and peas. An inventory of 1388 lists two cart-horses, a cart, ploughs, oxen, pigs and 48 cattle, but only five sheep.

Archaeology suggests this mixed farming economy of arable, pasture and meadow continued well into the late 15th century. But a gradual depopulation of the villages had begun, and by 1540, now under the ownership of the Tresham family, the villages and vibrant communities had almost vanished. This coincides with the Treshams obtaining a licence to empark 120 acres of wood, 250 acres of pasture and 50 acres of meadow, which had all been laid down to grass by 1544.

But later in the 16th century, instead of leasing the land, the Treshams began to farm the land and went into sheep-farming on a large scale.

By 1597 the Lyveden pastures held over 6,000 of Sir Thomas Tresham's sheep, and plans were afoot for converting Lyveden into a grand family seat.

The Tresham Family

Thomas Tresham was born into a wealthy and respected Northamptonshire family. His ancestors had come to Northamptonshire from Gloucestershire at the end of the 14th century, and in the 15th century were lifted out of the ranks of minor gentry by William Tresham and his son Thomas. William Tresham (d.1450), of Sywell near Northampton, was a lawyer and MP for Northamptonshire for many years. He was Attorney General under Henry V and three times Speaker of the House of Commons under Henry VI. Thomas (d.1471) served as Controller of Henry VI's Household, represented Northamptonshire in Parliament, and was Speaker of the House of Commons in 1460. William acquired large estates in Northamptonshire, among them the manor of Rushton. Thomas added other properties including the manor of Lyveden. Their houses at Rushton and Lyveden became the two main residences of the family.

William's grandson, Sir Thomas Tresham the elder (d.1559), served in the Protestant households of Henry VIII and Edward VI, but remained throughout a Catholic. He was therefore an ardent supporter of Mary Tudor, proclaimed Queen at Northampton in 1552, and was rewarded by her with the appointment of Grand Prior of the Order of St John of Jerusalem, when she restored that Order in England in 1557. It was only a brief appointment, however, as Mary died the next year, and Prior Thomas Tresham the year after. His son John had died before him, and so his heir was his grandson Thomas, aged only fifteen, but now head of a leading Northamptonshire family.

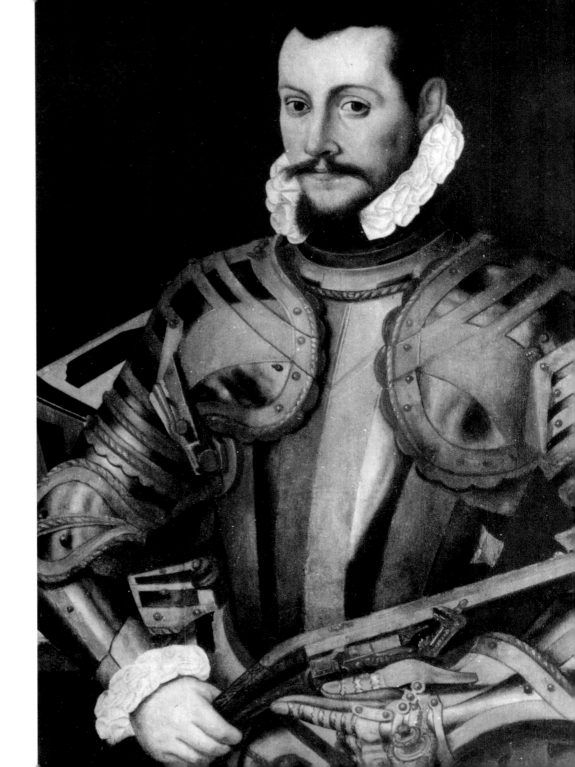

Right Sir Thomas Tresham
as a young man

'[A man] most Odious in the County'. WILLIAM CECIL'S AGENT ON SIR THOMAS TRESHAM, 1603

Clever and well educated, Thomas Tresham studied at Christ Church, Oxford and was admitted as a lawyer to the Middle Temple in 1560 at the age of only seventeen.

Tresham moved in the highest circles of county society. He was acquainted with his neighbours William Cecil, Secretary of State to Queen Elizabeth, and Sir Christopher Hatton, Lord Chancellor, who secured valuable positions at Court for members of the Tresham family. Both were influential builders of the period. Hatton's great houses at Holdenby and Kirby Hall and Cecil's Burghley House and Theobalds, each with complex gardens of terracing and moats, were at the forefront of modern design and architectural innovation. Tresham was knighted at the Queen's progress at Kenilworth in 1575, at the same time as Robert Cecil, future Earl of Salisbury and builder of Hatfield.

About 1566 Tresham married Muriel Throckmorton, a member of a prosperous Catholic family from Coughton Court in Warwickshire. Of their twelve children, nine survived – three sons and six daughters. Four of their daughters were married at considerable expense to peers or future peers. Sir Thomas's ruthless and efficient farming methods funded this expense. By 1590 Tresham was receiving at least £1,000 a year from tenants and a further £1,000 from his sheep. He sold horses at Market Harborough, hogs at Kettering and oxen at Coventry and Banbury. Under normal circumstances, this level of income would have supported a knight's family very adequately, even without the profits of state office. But Tresham's skill in managing his estates was not matched by

a similar efficiency in his personal affairs.

Sir Thomas enjoyed a lavish lifestyle. He entertained not only his friends and acquaintances, but their friends and followers 'to the number of twenty, forty, yea sometimes an hundred' (their names were often not known to him). He would feast upon over 50 cattle and 200 sheep in a single year. In ten months from Michaelmas 1588, accounts show that £456 15s 9d was spent in his kitchen.

In comparison, his building costs were relatively modest. Accounts from the 1590s show the largest expenditure in any year of £239 3s 9d in 1596, and the total for five years and seven months was only £971 0s 11d. Using local materials, practically all from his own land, kept costs down and meant that his building expenditure had little effect on his finances.

Below Coughton Court in Warwickshire, the family home of Tresham's wife, Muriel Throckmorton

Robert Winter · Bates · Christopher Wright · Iohn Wright · Thomas Percy · Guido Fawkes · Robert Catesby · Thomas Winter

Tresham's family posed the most significant financial burden. Up to and after his death in 1605, over £12,000 was given as marriage portions to his daughters. The reckless and unstable character of his son Francis was the major cause of Sir Thomas's financial difficulties. In 1593 Francis demanded £1,000 to settle fines, and again in 1601, when he was charged with treason, which cost £1,000 in bribes to Lady Katherine Howard and a fine of £2,000. His mother, Lady Tresham, was left to settle the penalty for Francis's part in the Gunpowder Plot to destroy the Houses of Parliament in 1605.

Thomas's religion also contributed to his impoverishment. At a time when Queen Elizabeth was threatened by the Catholic powers of Europe, led by Spain and by her imprisoned cousin Mary Queen of Scots, Catholic 'recusants' in England were targets for continual persecution.

The arrival of Jesuit missionaries in 1580 affirmed Tresham's faith in the Roman Catholic church. Alive to the dangers posed by his faith, he conveyed all his pastures and his stock to trustees for twelve years from 1581, drawing a modest yearly sum of £180 13s 4d. He was soon made an example to other Catholics of the powers of the state over the property of recusants. A conviction for refusing to attend the Anglican church was made on 20 December 1581, accompanied by a monthly fine of £20. This was affordable, and not exacted until 1587, but then he faced an arrears bill of over £950. Between 1581 and 1605, Tresham paid penalties totalling just under £8,000. He had insufficient surplus cash, so had to resort to borrowing. His credit never fully recovered.

Furthermore, for 25 years Tresham lived as a hostage, seized by the government whenever the machinations of Catholics abroad seemed to menace the safety of the realm. For a landowner who sought to direct all matters of estate management, this was a grave disability. Added to his frustration was a son and heir, deprived of parental control, embittered by his father's suffering, and ready to join in any desperate scheme against the government.

In spite of this unrelenting harassment, when Sir Thomas died on 11 September 1605, he was still a considerable landowner, but he left a debt of £11,495 16s 1d behind him. Francis inherited the estate, but found himself liable for his father's debts. This probably hastened his premature death, on 23 December 1605. While the estate now passed to Francis's younger brother Lewis, Lady Tresham shouldered the debt. For ten years she devoted the profits of the property and even her own goods and chattels to repaying it. Just before her death in 1615, only £1,000 of the debt remained. To cover this, she conveyed to Sir Thomas Brudenell of Deene her 1,092 sheep and the corn and hay on her Lyveden grounds.

Lewis was as reckless as his older brother, and despite becoming a baronet in 1611, his debts grew larger and larger. All that survives of his time at Lyveden is the remaining portion of the Old Bield, which was probably built by him as an addition to the older manor. Lewis's son William, who died childless in 1643, was the last of the main line of the Treshams. A junior line may have inherited Lyveden, but the estate had been sold by 1668.

Francis Tresham and the Gunpowder Plot

Francis was a latecomer to the conspiracy whom Robert Catesby, Tresham's cousin, hoped would rally Catholic support in the Midlands. But Tresham had many friends in the House of Lords, and, horrified by the violence of the plot, he tried to persuade Catesby to abandon it.

Francis proved to be the weak link in the chain of conspiracy. Although he was fanatical about his religion, foolish, rich, a gambler and in appalling financial trouble, he was also notoriously unreliable and indiscreet.

On 26 October 1605, Francis's brother-in-law, Lord Monteagle, received a letter urging him to 'retire yourself into the country for … they shall receive a terrible blow the Parliament and yet they shall not see who hurts them'. This letter – or at least the warning – is thought to have come from Francis Tresham. When it was passed to Robert Cecil, James I's secretary of state, the plot was unmasked. The leading conspirators were tortured and executed in the Tower, but Francis Tresham died before his trial. His head was removed and placed on a spike at the gates to Northampton, and his mutilated body was simply discarded.

Above Lyveden Old Bield in 1847

Right The Triangular Lodge at Rushton embodied Tresham's devotion to the Trinity in stone

Liberated from the need to build for defence by the establishment of domestic peace and financed by a buoyant economy, the Tudor aristocracy indulged in a frenzy of competitive building, which gradually changed the face of the countryside. Stimulated by the Elizabethan court, architecture became a matter of passionate interest and social rivalry characterised by symbolism, allegory and fantasy. Shakespeare was incorporating similar puzzles in his plays, while patrons such as Tresham, Hatton and Burghley were displaying ingenious conceits on their buildings.

Below The Market House at Rothwell

Tresham's first building was the Market House at Rothwell, the neighbouring town to his home at Rushton, where he was lord of the manor. Work started in 1578 under the direction of the mason William Grumbold. Friendship was the theme of the Market House, which displayed 90 coats of arms of local landed families. Latin inscriptions claim that it was the work of Sir Thomas 'as a tribute to his sweet Fatherland and County of Northampton but chiefly to this town his near neighbour … nothing but perpetual honour of his friends.' Sir Christopher Hatton, another near neighbour, gave the stone for building the Market House from his Weldon quarries. But work was interrupted by Tresham's arrest in 1580, and the building was roofed only in 1897.

Between 1593 and 1597 Tresham designed and built the Triangular Lodge on his Rushton estate (now in the care of English Heritage). Planned as an equilateral triangle, the gables, the windows and the numbers and devices inscribed on the building are all expressed in threes or multiples of three. Much smaller than the New Bield, the Triangular Lodge or 'warrener's lodge' was occupied by the keeper in charge of the Rushton rabbit warren, run by Tresham as a profitable commercial enterprise to supply the London markets.

Tresham's principal seat at Rushton Hall was extended and modernised in 1594/5, and the adjoining gardens were remodelled to create a series of large terraces, a spiral viewing mount and an extensive lake, which was achieved by damming the river.

Work commenced at Lyveden in 1594 and was still in progress when Tresham died in 1605. For much of this period he was under house arrest or in prison, and so was obliged to direct the work at Lyveden through letters to his agent.

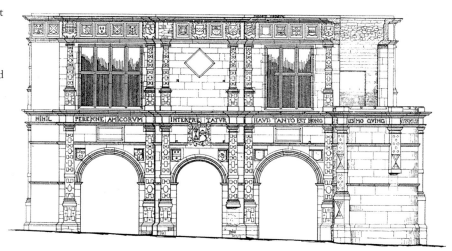

'The enriching of the friezes, I refer that unto you and the workmen.'

LETTER FROM ROBERT STICKELLS TO SIR THOMAS TRESHAM

Parris, who was a skilled stonemason from Norfolk, together with his assistant, undertook the detailed carving at both Lyveden and the Triangular Lodge.

William Grumbold had undertaken major building works at Rothwell Market House for Tresham. Tresham refers to him as 'old Grumbold' (presumably, his son was 'the other Grumbold'); together, they were responsible for providing the building materials, but always under the authority of Tresham himself.

Various other staff are mentioned by name including stone cutters Adams, Cunmingly and Raynes, and stonemasons Thomas Tyrrell, old Tyrrell and old Tyrrell's grandson. They were presumably employed at the quarry face, either at Pilton or at Weldon, which Tresham rented from Sir Christopher Hatton for the duration of his building works. The oolitic limestone was often roughly shaped at the quarry, as it became much harder when exposed to the atmosphere. Obsessed with detail and quality, Tresham ensured that stone of perfect strength and colour was chosen.

In the garden, Andrews was his nurseryman, who, as well as planting trees, was directed to visit London for plum stakes, and Gloucestershire, Worcestershire and Shropshire for pear and cider kernels.

Slynne and Levens were responsible for organising the large number of local labourers employed in the task of levelling the site with wooden spades, and shifting thousands of tonnes of spoil to construct the elaborate system of moats, mounts and terraces which still survives today.

Above right 17th-century gardeners at work, from the Rev. William Lawson's *A New Orchard and Garden*

Top Tresham directed operations from prison via detailed letters to his staff. This surviving fragment specifies varieties of fruit tree to be planted

Multi-discipline surveyors were employed in Elizabethan England, but specialist architects were beginning to emerge as a profession only at the end of the 16th century. Tresham corresponded regularly with Robert Stickells, who was employed by both Cecil and Hatton and described as an 'architect freemason'. However, the actual extent of Stickells's work at Lyveden is uncertain, as drawings exist in his hand in the Tresham papers for Hawkfield Lodge at Rushton, which no longer exists, but none for Lyveden. Tresham himself had considerable architectural knowledge, and many detailed drawings and calculations are in his own hand. He wrote at great length to his foreman John Slynne, giving precise measurements for the layout, and to his surveyor George Levens, directing how to draw out the plot for the building and gardens. Levens had also been responsible for the engineering work on the gardens at Rushton Hall.

Estate workers formed the majority of the workforce, but specialists were also employed.

Left The precision of the New Bield's stonework – still as crisp as the day it was carved – is a tribute to the skill of Tresham's stone cutters

21

Amazingly, Lyveden has stood as we see it today, undisturbed for over 400 years. Why was the lodge never completed, or the high-quality stone not removed for more useful buildings, or the canals not filled and garden mounds levelled to form additional farmland?

Half-hearted attempts to demolish Lyveden were made shortly after the Civil War, when Major General Boteler, a Cromwellian officer from Oundle, tried to use the building as a stone quarry. The solidity of Tresham's work defeated his efforts, and he had to be content with carrying away the roof beams, which are thought to have been incorporated into an Oundle schoolmaster's house.

The early history of Lyveden's ownership is rather vague. When the antiquarian John Bridges was writing his notes on Lyveden in 1721, it belonged to 'Sir Rowland Winn and Mr John Thornhaugh'. He describes a very similar setting to that we see today: 'It stands upon a ground in form of an amphitheatre with Woods round it except to the North and about a furlong to the East stands a pretty high mount … moated round with a broad deep moat'.

Lyveden was acquired by Lady Gowran in 1732. She was the granddaughter of Sir John Robinson, a former Lord Mayor of London, who in 1674 had bought the office of Master Forester and Keeper of Farming Woods. During this period the cottage was built, presumably from stone intended for the lodge and initially with

Top The east front in the mid-19th century

Above The south front, sketched in the early 18th century by Peter Tillemans

Right A postcard of the north front in the 1920s

a thatched roof. It was described as the 'Verderer's House', tenanted by the estate for the keeper of the Royal forest.

Lady Gowran married Richard Fitzpatrick, a naval officer of distinction who in 1740 commissioned a Dougald Campbell to complete the lodge, adding a second floor and domed roof. The plans were never executed, but still survive in the Northamptonshire Records Office.

The Fitzpatricks became the Earls of Upper Ossory, and the estate passed through the female line to the Lords Lyveden, who chose Farming (later Fermyn) Woods as the family home, leaving Lyveden virtually unchanged.

Lyveden remained in the ownership of the Fitzpatricks until the estate was broken up in the early 1900s. During the infancy of the National Trust, an appeal was co-ordinated by local dignitaries, including Earl Spencer and Alfred Gotch, to raise the £1,000 needed to buy Lyveden. Sir Ryland Adkins MP commented, 'It now happens that the opportunity has come for preserving for the public, and preserving against the attack of time, one of the most remarkable buildings in this country [and] one of the most instructive and important pieces of ground which could be found anywhere.' Sir Arthur de Capell Brooke added that 'he did not know of a more delightful place than Lyveden, at which jaded town workers could spend half a day.' The £1,000 target was achieved, and Lyveden was donated to the National Trust in 1922, safeguarding the property from the pressures of change through the decades that followed.

Only since the 1990s, however, has work begun on peeling back centuries of scrub and abandonment in order to preserve Lyveden for the next 400 years.

LYVEDEN BESIEGED
During May 1743, 98 soldiers of the Black Watch regiment barricaded themselves inside the moated garden at Lyveden, having rebelled against their officers following reports that they were to be sent to the West Indies. (Tropical disease meant that this was then a very unpopular posting.) After a siege lasting for several days, their resistance began to weaken. One soldier had died of hunger, and three others were executed as an example to the rest. Those who survived were marched back to London and posted overseas. On stormy nights, you are still supposed to be able to hear the pipes and drums of this Highland regiment.

Left Tenants of Lyveden cottage in the 1930s

23

THE GARDEN

'I have directed George [Levens, underforeman] how to draw the perimeter (or curcuit) of my Garden Plot wherein my garden lodge now standeth', wrote Sir Thomas Tresham from the confines of Ely prison to John Slynne on 9 October 1597.

The letter reveals Sir Thomas to have had a meticulously practical mind, as assiduous in his garden planning as he was in his farming and building plans. He was clearly a knowledgeable plantsman as well as a down-to-earth landscape architect.

Inspired by the great gardens of Europe, Tresham desired a garden filled with canals, terraces, viewing mounts and orchards. Essentially, his wishes still survive today.

Tour of the Garden
As you walk away from the lodge towards the moat, the scale and extent of the garden begin to unfold. At the highest point for some miles around, thousands of gallons of water are suspended in the clay-lined moats that encircle the former Middle Garden. The first question to arise is, where does the water come from? To which the answer is simple – rainfall. No spring or channels feed into the moats, only run-off from the surrounding banks and earthworks. The moats are only three or four feet deep, but perfect for stocking with fish and ideal for passing along in a boat. William Cecil's garden at Theobalds contained a similar ideal, with 'a ditch full of water, large enough for one to have the pleasure of going in a boat and rowing between the shrubs'.

The Spiral Mounts
The footbridge leads to one of the pair of spiral mounts in the garden. These features were extremely popular in 16th-century gardens, providing an elevated viewing point both over the garden and out into the landscape beyond.

At Wressle in Yorkshire, John Leland, a 16th-century traveller, describes 'mounds with a spiral flight of steps cut into them like the helix of a cockleshell, so that they could be climbed to the top without effort.' Similarly, at Dunham Massey in Cheshire, there was a 'circular mount in four stages'. Tresham had built a circular mount in the garden at Rushton, surmounted by a statue of Hercules. Adding stateliness to the garden, the mounts linked the formal garden within to the wider landscape beyond. At Lyveden this encompasses the former deer-park and hunting forest to the south and earlier sheep pastures to the north and east.

Below The very similar mount at Dunham Massey with its spiral path is clearly shown in John Harris's bird's-eye view of *c.*1750

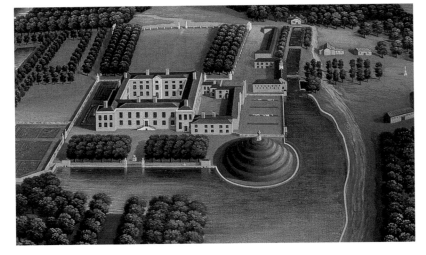

Above and left
Lyveden still preserves
the original mounts,
terraces and canals from
Tresham's formal garden

Above and right The canal

The Moated Garden

In 1597 Tresham instructed his staff to 'go ahead with pace the digging of the west side of the moated orchard'. Yet it is this side of the square which remains unfinished. However, he implies that the central area was to be planted with fruiting trees. A number of old varieties of plum and crab apple still survive along the edge of the canal which may relate to the original planting. Further evidence of planting comes from the bottom of the moats, where the silt contains pollen grains dating back 400 years. Flowers such as pinks and bur-marigold, and herbs including coriander, parsley and fennel can be identified, and may have been planted in anticipation.

This central area, surrounded by canals and with viewing mounds at each corner, offers the ideal canvas for an elaborate geometric design. The site is still visibly raised in the middle, presumably to aid drainage, but also providing an elevated stage. Underneath the soil there are significant deposits of gravel, possibly to be spread along pathways.

Early aerial photographs suggest a circular pattern with diagonal features, following the fashionable labyrinth designs of the period. Was this area to form a maze pattern surrounded with fruit trees and bordered with scented flowers and medicinal herbs? Hopefully, our future archaeology will help to reveal more of Tresham's work.

The Raised Terrace

This protects the Middle Garden from northerly winds, with two further pyramidal prospect mounds at either end giving a new perspective of the estate and garden. The spoil from the parallel moat was probably used to form the retaining terrace.

Again, this design was not unusual for the period. Similar terracing was used at Montacute in Somerset and at Risley in Derbyshire, where the terrace was also separated from the garden by a long narrow piece of water. At Lyveden, the original terrace still survives as it was planned 400 years ago. The terrace not only served as a dam, but also provided a screen, masking the ingenuity of the moated garden from the lower orchard and manor house. The terrace was also the equivalent of the long galleries in Elizabethan mansions – somewhere elevated and dry to walk along, while enjoying the view.

The views from the terrace or the prospect mounts at either end change the perception of the lower orchard. Tresham planned to lead his guests up the central avenue of walnut trees and on to the terrace and mounts where, looking back, they would enjoy the view over the fruit-filled trees and towards the manor house below. To the Elizabethans, this was an aerial view, three centuries before people were truly able to take to the skies.

Above The Raised Terrace

Below Ox-eye daisies carpet the lawn around the New Bield

The Orchard

The orchard combined pleasure and profit. Pleasant blossom-lined walks in the springtime gave way to a profitable enterprise in the autumn. Sadly, the premature abandonment of the garden in 1605 meant Sir Thomas never enjoyed its fruits. In 1609, four years after his death, Lady Tresham offered the trees to Robert Cecil for his gardens at Hatfield: 'I think no one can furnish you with more and better trees and of a fitter growth than this ground, for my late husband, as he did take delight, so did he come to great experience and judgement therein.'

You could still see the original holes in which the orchard trees were planted until the 1950s, when they were ploughed over; fortunately, they are recorded on old aerial photographs. Tresham listed many of these fruit trees in an appendix to his letter to John Slynne in 1597. 'Catshead', 'Harveys' and 'Winter Queening' were chosen varieties of apples, along with Windsor and Worcester pears, plus damsons, plums and cherries.

In 2002 the Trust began replanting the orchard, obtaining many of the original varieties from the National Collection of fruit trees at Brogdale. The trees have been grafted on to vigorous rootstocks, and planted according to Tresham's specification.

For Tresham, having a good range of fruit was partly a matter of status and partly a matter of necessity. Walnuts, for example, were valued not only for their nutritious nut, but also for the medicinal uses of their leaves, which were supposed to cure chilblains, acne and swollen glands, among other complaints. Pears symbolised good health, fortune and hope, and were supposed to stem bleeding and diarrhoea. Cherries were fruits of paradise, with many soothing and rejuvenating properties. Plums, ruled by Venus, were, according to the herbalist Thomas Culpeper, 'like women – some better, some worse', whereas when dried as prunes they might 'loosen the belly, procure appetite and cool the stomach'.

The virtues and values of apples are less fanciful to us today. But apples have always been the symbol of love and happiness as well as playing a vital part in gardens. Tresham required fresh fruit not only for the table, but also for drying, for wines and juices, and for cooking in numerous ways, plain and fancy.

The Meadows

Surrounding the historic gardens are over 16 hectares (40 acres) of meadows and pastures, nestling in the lee of the ancient hunting forests of Rockingham. These fields are now managed to preserve the important setting of Lyveden as well as to promote wildlife conservation in the area. The meadows were established between 1997 and 2000, reverting arable land to more traditional farming methods. The hay meadows are cut during late July, enabling the wildflowers and grasses to shed their seeds. Sheep then graze the pastures throughout the autumn, following methods of husbandry practised over hundreds of years.

Hedgerows are now being replanted, where they were removed less than 50 years ago. Old aerial photographs and estate maps help to identify the former boundary lines. Where old hedges have survived, traditional methods of coppicing and hedge-laying are being adopted to preserve these features for the future.

Far left 'Catshead' apples were among the varieties ordered by Tresham for Lyveden and recently replanted in the Orchard

Left and above
Lyveden from the air in the 1940s, when many of the ancient hedgerows still survived. The same view 50 years later (*above*) reveals a much barer landscape

Sir Thomas urged Slynne to shape the plants to ensure that his arbour hedges didn't 'grow thin at the bottom' or leggy. He projected eight large arbours for ornaments and for planting: 'Some of them may be converted to gardening as wherein to keep the choyse plantes, flowers etc.' We do not know what the 'choyse plantes' consisted of, but Tresham does go on to mention 'roses both damask and red'.

Rose petals had many uses apart from scenting the air in the garden. Gerard's *Herbal* (1597) compares damask roses favourably with other types, being 'of more pleasant smel, and fitter for meat and medicine'. Tresham adds that the 'dropping of roses will hinder nothing growing under them', specifying 'herbs, strawberries or the like'. Today primroses and violets cover the banks in springtime, with occasional wild roses and a mixture of old and gnarled trees.

TRESHAM'S GARDEN DESIGN

'All the alleys in my garden must be throughout laid all over a full foot deep of stone before it be gravelled, where thus floored it will be evermore dry.'

INSTRUCTION TO JOHN SLYNNE FROM SIR THOMAS TRESHAM, 1597

It was the mark of the new rich of the Elizabethan age to provide an ostentatious show in all their creations. They vied with each other to design ever more elaborate houses and gardens. Canals, terraces, viewing mounts and orchards became essential elements of these intricate fabrications, providing amusement, recreation and abundant crops.

In France and Italy the garden had long been regarded as an integral part of the country house design. Formal and informal areas were created to set off the house to best advantage, exploiting the natural topography, drainage and outlook. In 1440 the Italian Renaissance architect Alberti described how the 'element of surprise in views was to be achieved if possible by siting the villa high so that one climbs gently but steadily up through the garden then, reaching the villa, discovers all of the glories of the view'.

A French book of designs from the 1570s by Jacques Androuet Du Cerceau may have been the source of inspiration for Tresham's gardens at Lyveden. His account of the châteaux of France provides stylish diagrams of square moats, doglegged gardens and the positions of buildings within the château grounds. These volumes seem to have encouraged Tresham to remodel the valley side to incorporate terraces, orchards and watercourses, with the symbolic garden lodge at the summit. This entailed a detailed knowledge of the geology and the gardening possibilities of the site.

In his 1597 letter to John Slynne, Tresham specified the dimensions of the garden plot, 'wherein my garden lodge now standeth'. From the building, an area was to be staked out to 108 yards square and planted with twin rows of hawthorn hedging to make 'a private walk' around the garden lodge.

Far left In the background of this early 17th-century portrait of Elizabeth of Bohemia are a spiral mount and canal very similar to those at Lyveden

Below This recently discovered plan of William Cecil's London garden records a spiral mount and formal layout of the kind preserved at Lyveden

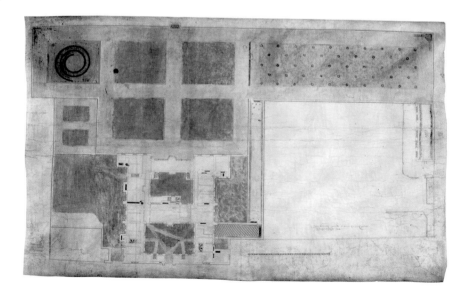

RESTORING THE GARDEN

'There are few gardens from this age that haven't been tampered with. I don't think even the National Trust realised what they had until they started clearing the scrub and found this virgin Elizabethan garden.' CHRIS BEARDSHAW, *BBC HIDDEN GARDENS*

A digital survey in 1996 revealed the outline of a garden obscured by centuries of neglect and abandonment. Property Manager Mark Bradshaw and his inspired team of volunteers set about stripping back the scrub and uncovering a garden lost in time.

Because of the sensitivity of the site, most of the clearance was undertaken by hand, almost in union with the men who laboured here 400 years ago. For many years you couldn't see the mounts for the trees, and the canals appeared to be no more than a series of discrete pockets of water interspersed with marshy patches of willow scrub.

In 1999 mechanical excavators were introduced to remove the silt from the canals, and slowly the site began to emerge. Most of the project work has been funded by donations and sponsorship, and the annual costs of maintaining Lyveden are now met by income generated at the property.

And the project continues. Fruit trees listed by Sir Thomas are now replanted in the orchard. Further clearance work is exposing more of the original garden form, and archaeology is gradually revealing how far Tresham's plans had progressed before being abandoned in 1605.

Right Brush-clearing during the recent restoration work on the garden